CULTURE
in the Kitchen

FOODS OF
China

By Therese Shea

Gareth Stevens
Publishing

Please visit our website, www.garethstevens.com. For a free color catalog of all our high-quality books, call toll free 1-800-542-2595 or fax 1-877-542-2596.

Library of Congress Cataloging-in-Publication Data

Shea, Therese.
Foods of China / Therese Shea.
       p. cm.— (Culture in the kitchen)
Includes index.
ISBN 978-1-4339-5704-8 (pbk.)
ISBN 978-1-4339-5705-5 (6-pack)
ISBN 978-1-4339-5702-4 (library binding)
1. Cooking, Chinese—Juvenile literature. 2. Food habits—China—Juvenile literature. 3. China—Social life and customs—Juvenile literature. I. Title.
TX724.5.C5S533 2011
641.5951—dc22

                                          2010046737

First Edition

Published in 2012 by
Gareth Stevens Publishing
111 East 14th Street, Suite 349
New York, NY 10003

Copyright © 2012 Gareth Stevens Publishing

Designer: Daniel Hosek
Editor: Therese Shea

Photo credits: Cover, pp. 1, 4, 5 (both images), 6, 7, 9, 10 (both images), 11, 12, 13, 14, 15 (both images), 18, 19, 20, 21 (all images) Shutterstock.com; p. 17 Billy Hustace/Photographer's Choice/Getty Images.

Printed in the United States of America

CPSIA compliance information: Batch #CS11GS: For further information contact Gareth Stevens, New York, New York at 1-800-542-2595.

Contents

Words in the glossary appear in **bold** type the first time they are used in the text.

All About China

China is a large country in east Asia. In fact, China is the largest country in the world! It has many different **regions**. There are mountains and valleys. It has deserts and rainy areas, too.

China also has the most people of any nation. It's home to many different **cultures**. These cultures value different foods. You may think you know what Chinese food is, but you probably haven't tried the most interesting and unusual dishes eaten in China. Read on to find out!

Another Bite

Chinese fortune cookies are treats with a written message inside. However, they were first made in the United States, not China.

◀ Shanghai (at left) is the largest city in China. The Great Wall of China (above) stretches more than 5,000 miles (8,045 km).

A Balanced Meal

Chinese meals balance different tastes. Something hot is served with something cold. A spicy food is offered with a mild dish. Some Chinese foods even use a sauce called "sweet and sour."

The Chinese meal is usually made up of two parts. The main part of the meal is a grain, such as rice, noodles, or a bun. The rest of the meal is made up of smaller dishes of vegetables, fish, or meat.

Meals are eaten with chopsticks, though spoons are used for soups.

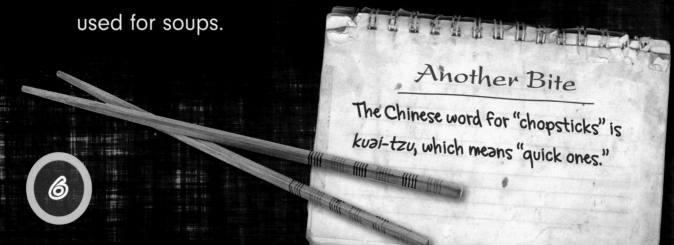

Another Bite

The Chinese word for "chopsticks" is *kuai-tzu*, which means "quick ones."

◀ Peking duck has been a Chinese speciality for over 400 years. The meat is covered in a sweet and spicy hoisin sauce.

Chinese Cuisines

There are many different kinds of Chinese **cuisines**. The eight most famous cuisines are Shandong, Guangdong, Sichuan, Hunan, Jiangsu, Zhejiang, Fujian, and Anhui. These cooking styles began in certain areas of China. Even neighboring regions may have very different cuisines. Geography, historic events, and the available **ingredients** made these differences possible. For example, areas near bodies of water use more fish in their cuisine than areas far from water. Part of the Shandong region lies on the Bohai Gulf and Yellow Sea. Shandong chefs are known for their excellent seafood dishes.

The Chi[...] have b[...] growing [...] in fields [...] this on[...] more [...] 8,000 y[...]

Another Bite

Sichuan (or Szechuan) cuisine is known for spicy food that uses chili peppers. Peanuts are used in the region's famous kung pao chicken.

Common Ingredients

When you order Chinese food in the United States, you probably receive rice or noodles, vegetables, and meat. These foods aren't too unusual to us. A more unusual vegetable you may find is bok choy, which is a kind of white cabbage. Vegetables called water chestnuts also offer an extra crunch in many dishes.

In recent years, tofu has become part of American cuisine. It's made from the liquid of soybeans. It was first made over 2,000 years ago in northern China. Edamame has become a popular soybean snack around the world.

bok choy

water chestnuts

◀ Tofu takes on the taste of the food and spices it's cooked with.

Unusual Ingredients

Meals prepared in China may have much more unusual ingredients than the foods we find in a local Chinese restaurant. Some dishes use turtle, snake, and snail meat. Many **traditional** dishes feature bamboo shoots.

bamboo shoots

Have you ever heard of a hundred-year egg? This special food isn't really that old. However, it's at least 100 days old! Hundred-year eggs are first coated with several ingredients. Then they're buried in the ground for 100 days. After they're dug up, the shells are removed. If prepared correctly, the eggs taste like cheese!

When hundred-year eggs are ready to be eaten, their shells turn black.

Another Bite

You can find hundred-year eggs in Chinese markets. They're also called century eggs or thousand-year eggs.

Foods with Stories

Some Chinese dishes became popular through stories. For example, West Lake **Braised** Fish in Vinegar is a famous dish of Zhejiang cuisine. A tale tells of a young fisherman who became very ill. His sister-in-law caught a fish and specially prepared it with vinegar and sugar. It made him better! Soon many people made fish the same way.

Fujian cuisine features a soup called **Buddha** Jumping over the Wall. It got its name because it was said to be so tasty that the holy man jumped over a wall to eat it!

wolfberries

Another Bite

The wolfberry is a tart red fruit used in Chinese cooking. The fresh berries can't be touched by hand or they'll turn black!

◀ The sweet longan fruit of China is also called dragon's eye. Dragons are a part of many Chinese stories.

Stir-Fry

The Chinese people have many ways of cooking. Steaming, frying, and baking are among them. Now popular everywhere, stir-frying was a method first used in China. Years ago, many Chinese stoves featured a hole over a burning fire. A **wok** fit over the hole and was heated by the fire. A small amount of oil and chopped food were then stirred in the pan. Stir-frying involves high heat and little oil. Stir-fried foods are cooked quickly, yet still keep their fresh taste and healthy qualities.

Some chefs let the oil in the wok catch fire, which cooks the food even faster.

17

Dim Sum

Dim sum is a traditional Chinese meal. It's served in late morning or early afternoon. Instead of diners ordering from a menu, servers push carts around the restaurant. Diners choose which foods they would like from the cart. Common foods include **dumplings**, steamed buns, spring rolls, and meat such as spareribs and chicken feet. Diners can try a bit of everything. The meal should be relaxing and take a long time. Accompanying dim sum is the most important drink in China—tea.

Another Bite

Spring rolls got their name because they were first made from spring vegetables. These are wrapped in a paper-thin covering of rice and then fried.

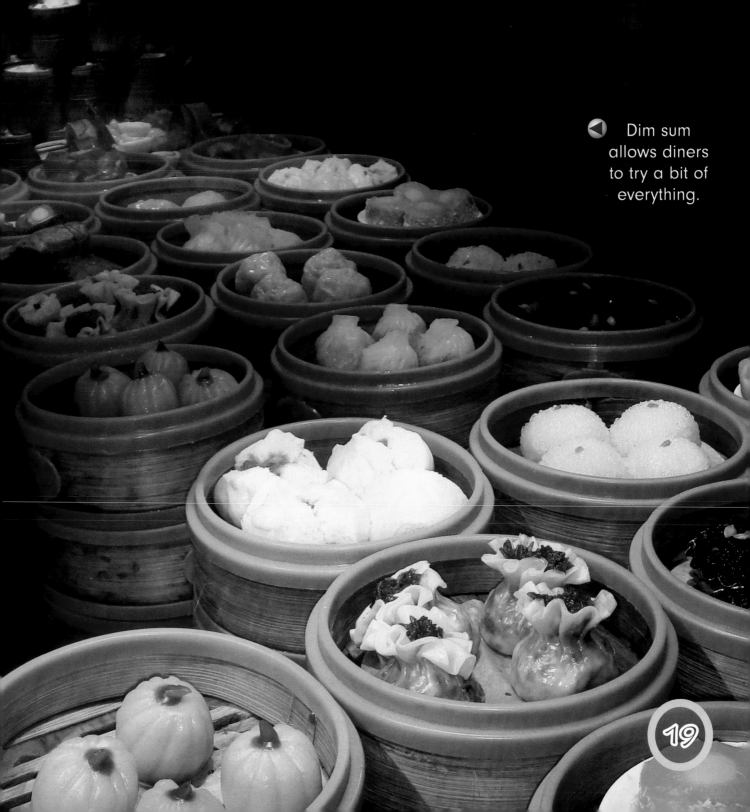

Dim sum allows diners to try a bit of everything.

19

Tea

For more than 4,000 years, the Chinese have been drinking tea. At first, people boiled tea leaves in water and used the drink as a medicine. Around AD 300, it became an everyday drink. The tea plant grew to be an important crop. The drink is made from its buds and young leaves.

Chinese tea spread to other countries, reaching Europe by 1610. Today, tea is the second-most popular drink in the world, behind water. Truly, China has given us many of our favorite things to eat and drink!

The age of the tea leaves ▶ determines the taste and name of the tea.

Recipe:
Stir-Fry Baby Bok Choy
(requires the help of an adult)

Ingredients:

4 bunches baby
bok choy

2 slices ginger

2 tablespoons
soy sauce

1 teaspoon sugar

1/4 teaspoon salt

1/4 cup water

A few drops sesame oil

1 1/2 tablespoons
vegetable oil

Directions:

1. Wash the baby bok choy. Separate the stalks and leaves. Cut the stalks **diagonally** and cut the leaves across.

2. Heat a wok (or another pan) and add oil. When the oil is hot, add the ginger and stir-fry for about 30 seconds.

3. Add the bok choy stalks first, and then the leaves. Stir in the soy sauce, sugar, and salt, and stir-fry on high heat for 1 minute.

4. Add the water, cover the wok, and cook for about 2 minutes. Stir in the sesame oil and serve. Serves 4.

Glossary

braised: describing a food that has been browned for a short time and then cooked in water at a low heat

Buddha: a spiritual teacher of ancient India who founded a way of life known as Buddhism

cuisine: a style of cooking

culture: the beliefs and ways of life of a group of people

diagonally: slanting from one side to another

dumpling: a small ball of dough, sometimes with food inside

ingredient: a part of a mixture

region: a large area of land that has features that make it different from other areas of land

traditional: having to do with long-practiced customs

wok: a large, thin metal pan with a curved bottom

For More Information

Books

Goodman, Polly. *Food in China*. New York, NY: PowerKids Press, 2008.

Hibbert, Clare. *China*. Minneapolis, MN: Clara House Books, 2010.

Websites

ChineseFood-Recipes.com: Glossary of Ingredients
www.chinesefood-recipes.com/glossary_of_ingredients/glossary_ingredients.php
Read about the many ingredients used in Chinese recipes.

Chinese Recipes
chinesefood.about.com/od/chinesecookingbasics/a/chinese_recipes.htm
Make Chinese meals at home with the help of the links on this website.

Index